Spontaneous Manifestations From Zero

Spontaneous Manifestations From Zero

Tapping Into The Universal Flow

Richard Dotts

1st Edition
ISBN-13: 9781522875024
ISBN-10: 1522875026
Questions / comments? The author can be contacted at
RichardDotts@gmail.com

Table of Contents

Chapter One

Accessing the Giant Universal Lever that Creates Worlds

It feels so wonderful to be back at my writing desk working on this next book. The thought of sharing my ideas and touching the lives of people from all over the world, almost all of whom I've never physically met, energizes me immensely. Of course, I don't usually get this sentimental at the start of each new book I write, but this time is different. I've just spent the past month traveling across two continents, which necessitated a break in my rigorous writing schedule. However, I more than made up for that lost time by partaking in wonderful new experiences and meeting beautiful people. I saw these Universal principles reflected back to me everywhere I turned, even in a foreign country.

My recent travels caused me to realize how far I have come in doing all of this inner work. The old Richard would not have allowed himself to drive in a foreign country for fear of getting into road accidents, but the new Richard did so without any incident and enjoyed himself tremendously!

The old Richard would not have allowed himself to travel light and trust that all his needs would be provided for on such a long journey, but the new Richard enjoyed the spontaneity of it all, and delighted in having his needs met by the Universe in extraordinary ways. The old Richard would not have believed that friendly, helpful people were ready to help at every corner of the street, even in the most "unfriendly" of places, but that was exactly what the new Richard experienced.

I can go on and on about this newfound freedom and life of mine, but you get the idea. Freedom, not from others or from the perceived problems in my life, but from my own negative programming and worrisome thoughts of the past. Freedom from the social conditioning and beliefs that I have unknowingly accepted throughout my life. Putting these spiritual principles into practice has liberated me from the irrational fears that gripped me in the past. I now see those fears for what they are, as baseless thoughts that are not grounded in truth. I am now free to perceive and enjoy life as it is meant to be, and so can you if you follow the steps outlined in these books.

As I look back at the changes in my own inner state, I realize that there is nothing particularly profound or groundbreaking about the steps I took. I did not take any particularly drastic steps in a single day. I did not cast a magic spell or wave a magic wand for all my manifestations to happen at once. Instead, I took things one step at a time. The ensuing results have been equally dramatic. When you demonstrate even the slightest willingness to change and signal your new intention in the smallest of ways, the Universe responds and reciprocates in a big way. This is how it feels to be part of the greater Universal flow. You have constant access to the powerful leverage provided by a giant Universal lever! No tremendous physical effort or willpower is necessary. All you have to do is to be *willing* to entertain a new reality. The moment you do, things happen spontaneously in your life (and on your behalf) that leads you to that desired reality. This is perhaps the greatest "secret" of the Universe.

Physical hard work and labor have never been part of the creative equation. If they *were* indeed crucial ingredients for manifestation, we would have achieved all our desired goals through sheer hard work alone. We would have solved all the problems of mankind through sheer physical effort. But why is it that despite our best efforts and despite putting long hours into "worrying" about various problems, that solutions continue to elude us? Perhaps we are looking in the wrong place for answers. What we need is a new way of looking at things—a new paradigm and a new level of consciousness.

Readers who read spiritual books often find things happening or manifesting for them spontaneously with no effort on their part. The magic seems to unfold as they read. To the beginner, this seems like pure coincidence or serendipity, but I can assure you that there are no coincidences in this Universe.

Everything in your life is here for a reason. You may have heard this clichéd saying countless times, but it is true. There is a reason why everything in your life is where it is. This is usually not a profound reason with a long romantic backstory, as many would like to believe, but a simple one: Everything in your life is here because you have attracted it in some way through the attractive power of your thoughts, feelings and beliefs.

Your repeated thoughts, feelings and beliefs about a situation give rise to your continued focus, which then perpetuates reality the way it is. Thankfully, any version of reality is not cast in stone. The moment you entertain the possibility of an alternative reality, you set powerful energetic forces into motion that cause things to shift for yourself. Understanding this Universal principle can mean the difference between living a comfortable life of effortless ease and one of constant head-on struggle. I have seen individuals (including myself) struggle their way through life and attract one unpleasant scenario after another simply because of their unwillingness to entertain the possibility of an alternative reality. Only you can make this life-changing choice for yourself.

We see this self-sabotaging pattern playing itself out in many areas of our lives. Individuals may read self-help books and then immediately decide that the ideas will never work for them. They may find fault with the content, writing, examples given or techniques shared. No matter how valid their reasoning or rebuttals may be, these individuals are often unconscious about the self-sabotaging behavior that has occurred at a fundamental level. Through their numerous criticisms and rejections of the work, they are refusing to entertain (even for a moment) an alternative reality where this might / could work for them. Their refusal to entertain these alternative possibilities in their minds is *precisely* the reason why things remain stuck for them.

I know this scenario only too well. Before I created lasting results in my life, I spent one decade (and lots of money) jumping from one technique, book or course to another. After learning about each new technique, I would be able to point out precisely the reasons why that technique "would not work for me," or how the teachings were so fundamentally flawed in more ways than one. Of course, my criticisms of the material were perfectly valid to me, but they also meant another thing: I was doomed to failure even before I began! I absolutely refused to entertain the possibility of success even in my mind's eye! I was using my own faulty conditioning and past experiences to justify why things would always turn out the same way.

This is the key—had I suspended my own judgment back then <u>for even one moment</u> and given the material some consideration, things would have happened for me no matter what "technique" or "method" I used. As I now understand today, most of the techniques and methods offered out there are a *bridge* for us to access alternative realities, by offering us easy (and acceptable) ways to change our inner states.

These techniques offer an easy way for us to transition from one way of thinking and being into another by providing an impetus or platform for us to do so. Therefore, it is often not the techniques themselves that bring about the corresponding results in our outer reality, but our new inner states that produce the results.

Let me illustrate this with three possible scenarios. See if you can identify yourself in any of them.

Apathetic Ann reads a book about creating more financial abundance in one's life in which the author shares a series of steps to do so. Ann, who is skeptical about such methods, refuses to entertain any possibility that the ideas could work for her. Not only does she not try anything from the book, reading it makes her feel worse because her own financial situation becomes even more apparent to her. She starts to see everything as a scam. Thus, the book has the *opposite* effect on Ann from what is intended: It amplifies her own feelings of financial lack and leads to negative feelings of resentment over her situation, which of course leads to more lack in her outer reality.

Enthusiastic Ernest reads the same book and feels all excited by the ideas shared within. However, Ernest has a habit of jumping from one book and technique to another, searching for that missing "secret" that will finally work. The difference between Apathetic Ann and Enthusiastic Ernest is that while

Ann is vocal with her criticisms about the material, the blocks for Ernest occur at an unconscious level. On the surface, Ernest is enthusiastic and hopes that these ideas will finally work to produce results in his life. But he is also secretly doubtful because similar books have not produced results in the past. At the level of his unconscious beliefs, Ernest is holding on to beliefs about failure and things not working out. He reads the book with an overwhelming sense of self-doubt. Guess what happens when he tries to apply the material? His overriding feelings of worry and self-doubt form his dominant intent, which can only lead to corresponding negative results.

Now comes Neutral Nat, who is not affected by anything that has happened in the past. Neutral Nat reads the same book with a *zero* state of mind—with absolutely no expectations for the future, or thoughts and feelings from the past or present. This does not mean that Neutral Nat has *no* past. It simply means that he is free from the influences of everything that has happened before in his experience. He reads the book with a clean slate, with no expectations, judgments or attachments to the outcome. Because he is not affected by anything from the past or present, Neutral Nat is not sabotaged by his own negative programming. If he decides to try a technique or new method from the book, he is able to implement it in his life purely and see the desired results quickly. Even if Nat were to just sit on the ideas in the book *without* putting any of them into action, things would still happen for him because the mere act of *reading* that book would have allowed him to access a better-feeling inner state of financial abundance and prosperity. Just holding that inner state purely in his consciousness without any contradictory negative feelings would lead to positive physical outcomes, by virtue of the Law of Attraction.

Now here's the kicker—Apathetic Ann, Enthusiastic Ernest and Neutral Nat are all the same person. There is a bit of them in each of us. Before I recognized my infinite potential, I was Apathetic Ann, someone who refused to believe that any of this was possible. Once I tasted some success and was eager for more, I became Enthusiastic Ernest trying to connect the dots and make things work, while not entirely believing that they would. I kept moving back and forth between being Apathetic Ann and Enthusiastic Ernest, depending on what I observed in my outer reality until I finally realized that the way to produce lasting results in my world was to be as neutral as Nat.

You too, can decide to become Neutral Nat at any time. It is a state that you gradually *practice* yourself into. It is a conscious decision that you make. The more you practice being in that neutral state of zero, the better you become at it.

This means putting yourself into an inner state of mind that is conducive to outer manifestations. This means freeing yourself from your own expectations, preconceived notions, fears, judgments and beliefs of what is possible, or what *should* rightfully happen. It means freeing yourself from any logical rationalizations or thoughts. Of course, all of this is easier said than done. But once you learn how to access and remain in this *mindless* state where there are no judgments, no thoughts and no feelings...that is when all the miracles and manifestations happen for you. This is the state of spontaneous manifestations. It does not exist at some point in the future. It exists right now, within you. Once you get there, it does not matter what technique or method you use. Things *just* happen for you, with you as a conscious observer reveling in the absolute perfection of it all.

It is my intention with this book to show you how to get there in the fastest way possible, and stay there for most of the time!

Chapter Two

Apply the Magic Transformation Process for Fast Results

Before we begin our journey together, I would like to share an important insight that I gleaned while on my recent trip. Realizing this insight will make things much easier for you, no matter where you are on the spiritual path. I had plenty of time to contemplate and ponder while on my recent travels. Much of it was done in those cramped airline seats where I simply could not do anything else but explore the richness of my inner world!

And so while I was "trapped" in one of those tightly confined spaces waiting to go somewhere, I started looking back at my own spiritual and personal development journey. When did it all begin, and what were some of the things I did along the way that really made the greatest difference for me? What were some of the things I inadvertently did that slowed me down?

Readers of my other books will know that things really started happening for me when I managed to let go of my worrisome and fear thoughts that plagued me for most of the day. When I was still my former self, I would worry the moment I woke up in the morning right to the point I fell asleep at night. I had trouble falling asleep on most nights because I was literally worrying myself into insomnia! This self-defeating cycle continued for years. Looking at the imaginary course I charted in my mind, I realized that massive changes occurred once I let go of most of my negative fear thoughts. That was the decisive turning point where most of the outer changes occurred.

Next, I looked back at all of the spiritual teachers who had touched my life in one way or another. I had many of them, most of whom taught me through their written words. It was then I realized that each and every teacher had something special to offer to me, although I could not always see their value at that point in time. More importantly, all of the teachers whom I attracted into my life were teaching the *truth.* What differed were the ways in which they communicated this truth, and also the ways they shared to enable us to discover this truth for ourselves.

What struck me as particularly interesting was that while I had heard Abraham-Hicks say the same thing over and over again for years, it took me 10 years (!) before I was able to take what they were saying and apply it successfully in my own life. Once I applied what they taught, I never looked back. Things changed for me forever.

The main teaching of Abraham-Hicks is that you get what you focus on by virtue of the Law of Attraction. If you continue to tell the same old story of what you do not want, then you are going to continue getting what is undesired in your life. However, the moment you start telling a new story, the moment you tell the story of how you would like things to be, that is when changes start happening for you. Such simple teachings expressed in two sentences, yet I took one decade to fully internalize and master them! Why is that so?

Now that I have been on both sides as a student and teacher, I recognize this as the missing piece that trips most people up in their application of this material. I realize it is because most of us fail to **apply the Magic Transformation** to each new teaching that we come into contact with. Once you learn how to apply the Magic Transformation to each new teaching you are introduced to, the intended results will happen faster and more effectively in your life than ever before. Let me explain further.

All of us are at different points along our spiritual journey. As a result, we meet with these teachings at different levels of consciousness and prior understanding. It would be best if we all came to the table with an entirely clean slate, but that is rarely the case. Each of us brings along the emotional baggage of our past experiences, the sum total of our expectations, and also our conscious and unconscious attachments to the outcome. This makes it difficult for us to perceive what these teachers communicate purely without tainting their message with some form of our own bias.

Another reason is that spiritual teachers are usually at an elevated level of consciousness, having practiced and realized this material for themselves. They have done the inner work necessary while we are merely looking in from the other side, not having experienced any of it for ourselves. This is especially the case for non-physical beings, such as Abraham, who do not perceive the same physical limitations as humans do from our everyday perspective.

Hence, when Abraham-Hicks talk about the importance of "feeling good" and "telling a new story," they often do not have to deal with the physical resistance in the process that makes this difficult for the rest of us. For example, individuals who have tried to "feel good" or visualize their desired outcomes in the face of unpleasant situations will know that it is extremely difficult to do so. We just cannot stop the momentum of our negative thoughts at once. Being human makes it difficult for us to drop all of our negative thoughts and feelings at once and focus on a desired outcome, but these same physical limitations do not present themselves to non-physical beings. Thus, while we *know* what we have to do, putting the steps into actual practice can be challenging because of the obstacles that crop up along the way for us.

This issue presents itself in another way when we try to learn some form of spiritual healing. Spiritual healers are usually talented individuals who have found a way to access and direct healing abilities for themselves or others spontaneously. They usually have difficulties teaching or communicating the process to others, simply because the whole process happens so intuitively for them! They often do not think of the process in a step-by-step, linear fashion, neither do they vocalize each step in words. They just do it! When it comes to accessing these healing energies, there is nothing they have to strive hard towards or figure out in order for the healing to take place.

However, teaching the process to others is another story altogether. These talented healers are now forced to use physical actions, steps and words to represent what they do on the inside. They are forced to give each step some form of literal meaning. Thankfully, many of them are also masterful teachers, which is why many of these teachings *do* get replicated by others.

But even if teachers are masterful at communicating what they know, the rational, reasoning minds of students usually interfere with the learning process. Students often want to know the purpose or reason behind each step instead of just *doing* it directly. This act of thinking and trying to "rationalize" each step sabotages most of our efforts to learn spiritual healing or other forms of intuitive ability.

It is not because these abilities cannot be effectively taught. Rather, it is because they cannot be effectively taught in conventional ways. We unknowingly distort these teachings even before we apply them.

If you're like me, your bookshelf may be filled with hundreds of metaphysical books on spiritual healing or various forms of esoteric techniques. The majority of those who read these books never see any results from them, which is a pity because all of these books teach some form of truth! Before I realized these principles for myself, I was disappointed each time I read a spiritual healing book, only to discover that I could not replicate the amazing results or steps for myself. But the moment I applied the **Magic Transformation** to each technique I learned, results happened so quickly and spontaneously that it was as if I was another person altogether! Let's take a look at the **Magic Transformation** process and how it works.

In a nutshell, the **Magic Transformation** process takes the teachings as presented by a spiritual teacher in their original form and ***transforms*** those teachings into a form that is understandable, relatable and accessible by you. The transformation that takes place with this information will differ from one person to the next. When we do not deliberately apply the **Magic Transformation** process, we often end up distorting that information anyway to suit our current understanding. This is where the pitfall is. You have to *consciously* transform the information in a way that can be readily applied by you before your unconscious perceptual filters and beliefs kick in. Once they do, the essence of these messages will be lost.

Let me take you through the **Magic Transformation** process. You repeat this process with each new teaching or body of spiritual knowledge that you are exposed to. You apply the transformation process by asking a series of simple questions. The aim of these questions is to get your rational, reasoning self out of the way and focus on the core essence of the teachings themselves. You'll find that the Magic Transformation process can be applied to *any* book, method or technique that you are exposed to, especially those in which the teachers have not managed to explain their philosophy as clearly in words.

The first question to ask after you have read the entire book or been introduced to the whole system of teachings is this:

(1) In a few words or a single sentence, what would a 5 year old learn to do from this book, technique or method?

The purpose of this first question is to get you to think literally about the message. It is actually a clever way of getting you to drop all your past understanding and experience, and focus on the core of the current teachings themselves. We often think we have beneficial past experiences to bring to the table, when in fact these past experiences often interfere with our integration of new material. This first question starts you off on a clean slate.

When I ask this question about the teachings of Abraham-Hicks, I intuitively know that the answer is "to stop worrying about what I do not want and feel good." The literal interpretation of Abraham-Hicks' teachings is that we should feel good, as simple as that!

When I ask the same question about more "advanced" esoteric teachings, such as Matrix Energetics (which by the way, many people have trouble wrapping their heads around), the answer to a 5 year old would be: To drop into the heart space and do the 2-point (which is a technique taught in Matrix Energetics).

When you ask the same question about an energy healing technique, the answer to a 5 year old could be: To run my hands over the injured area while feeling the energy. As simple as that!

The intention here is to convey the core essence of these teachings in as few words as possible. The more words we use, the more associated thoughts we have and the more rationalization of the process takes place. Remember that the point here is to cut out any unwanted rationalization of the process.

The second question to ask is:

(2) Am I doing it? Yes or No.

This is a simple Yes or No question. The answer is either a clear Yes or a clear No. There are no qualifiers or in-betweens, and "no...but" is certainly not an acceptable answer!

For example, when I ask the second question as it is applied to the teachings of Abraham-Hicks ("Am

I doing it? Have I stopped worrying about what I do not want and do I feel good?"), the answer I would have given in the past is a clear no! I *thought* I was applying their teachings, but in fact I wasn't. I was merely applying a distorted version of their teachings to fit my own beliefs, not as they had intended it, but as my *own belief system* had intended. My own belief system distorted the message even before I had a chance to apply it properly. This is why I missed out on the results.

The second question gets you to face the truth and realize that you have <u>not</u> been applying these teachings all this while. What you might have been doing was to merely read about them and talk about ways in which they could not possibly work for you. We want to skip all of that self-defeating behavior here that can hold people back.

The third question to ask is:

(3) If no, what am I doing instead?

Take a good look at how you are applying the teachings in your own life. Are you doing anything with them? If I had taken the time to go through this simple series of questions, my answer to this third question back then would have been: While I am constantly reading about these spiritual principles, I am still actively holding on to my worry and fear thoughts.

With that answer, the discrepancy between the teachings and my actual behavior would have become obvious to me. It is important to answer these questions frankly and truthfully. Take a close look at what and how you are applying these teachings in your daily life, then write down in a single sentence how you have been applying them. Your answers will hold the keys to your results (or lack of results).

For example, an individual who has trouble learning a spiritual healing technique may answer: "I have been running my hands over the injured area, but instead of feeling the energy, my mind is filled with thoughts of whether I am doing it right." That is a common one for individuals who are trying to learn a new spiritual healing technique!

What we do next is to compare our answers to questions (1) and (3). The discrepancy gives you an indication as to where you may have stumbled into a pitfall. That's why it is recommended to write down your answers to these questions to avoid shifting them around in your mind. Your rational mind will shift the answers around to rationalize its actions if you attempt to do this exercise all in your mind. Write the answers down on paper in the form of short sentences.

(1) What would a 5 year old do after learning this process? "To run my hands over the injured area while feeling the energy."

(2) Am I doing it? No.

(3) What am I doing instead? "I am running my hands over the injured area, but instead of feeling the energy, my mind is filled with thoughts of whether I am doing it right."

The final question is:

(4) What do I need to do to close the gap or reduce the difference?

You'll see that in this example, the "gap" between theory and practice is that the students' minds are filled with constant thoughts about whether they are doing it right. These thoughts in turn give rise to feelings of worry and self-doubt. Therefore, an insightful transformation has just taken place here that is of great value. What these particular students need to do, *on top of* applying the energetic healing teachings as taught, is to find a way to quiet their minds and remove any thoughts of whether they are doing it right. This is an additional step that these particular students have to take to ensure their successful application of the material. Of course, this is just an example, and you will find once you apply the Magic Transformation for yourself that new insights are often gained. For example, you may not know you have been unconsciously sabotaging your own progress in this way until the discrepancy is revealed by answering the Magic Transformation questions.

As you practice the Magic Transformation process, you'll automatically approach each new teaching or body of knowledge with a clean slate. Soon, you will catch yourself even before you begin, which means you do not have to consciously ask and go through the four questions every time. But I still go through these four questions each time I find myself struggling even a little bit with integrating a new method into my life. When I bring myself through these four simple questions, I often realize that it is either something I have learned in the past, an existing resistant thought or an existing unconsciously held belief that is interfering with my current results. When I let that go, the intended results happen for me spontaneously.

Summary of the 4 **Magic Transformation** questions: (Answer each question in one sentence or less).

(1) What would a 5 year old learn to do from this method?
(2) Am I doing it? Yes/No.
(3) What am I doing instead?
(4) What is the difference/gap? How can I close it?

Chapter Three

Moving Away from the Band-Aid Approach to Manifestations

In the previous chapter, I shared the simple Magic Transformation process that you can use to increase your own conscious awareness when learning a new spiritual technique or skill. I wanted to share the process early on in this book so you can use it immediately with the teachings that follow, or with any metaphysical process or material that you come into contact with.

If you have been on this path for quite some time, your bookshelf will invariably be filled with spiritual books of all types, from the pragmatic to the esoteric. I should know because I have quite a collection of metaphysical books myself and find great joy in adding new books to my collection every now and then! Even though I am less zealous about adding new material to my library nowadays, I find myself integrating and applying each new teaching into my life in a more complete way. I no longer move from one book to another or from one technique to another hoping to find that "golden key."

Instead, I recognize that *all* of them hold their own golden keys, and collectively, these teachings have the power to create exciting changes in my life.

If you have been tearing through one book or course after another in search of that elusive "golden key," or if you find yourself setting books aside in disappointment because the steps do not work as claimed, maybe it is time to revisit those materials that you have set aside and apply the Magic Transformation process to each of them. Take a close look at the teachings and identify where or how you have deviated from them. How have you unknowingly added your own spin on things? Very often, adding your own "spin" distorts the material such that you are unable to create progress in your life.

After realizing what I had done to self-sabotage my own learning process in the early days and developing the Magic Transformation process, I made it a point to revisit all the old books that I had read and set aside. Don't turn this into a chore or a rushed affair. Instead, it is a good idea to pick up old books once in a while and see what you can glean from them. You may think you already know everything that is inside, but the memory is often spotty. What we pick up from an earlier reading might have corresponded to our earlier level of consciousness. When we meet with these familiar teachings at a new level of consciousness, we are often surprised by what new takeaways or dimensions we may discover from the work. This is true with any teaching.

I enjoy picking up old books from time to time and either reading them through in their entirety or reading snippets to see if any of them ring a bell. Very often, the snippets take on a completely new interpretation and bring about a completely new world of possibilities for me. For example, I love reading the Seth books and each new reading brings about new discoveries. Often, I find myself nodding in agreement as I read, thinking "Oh, *now* I finally understand what Seth was trying to convey back then!" If you stop thinking of the words on a page as static, you'll start to see them as portals to alternative worlds and alternative dimensions.

Any student of manifestation is trying to traverse between two worlds. First, there is the world in which the student is familiar. We call this the current reality. And next, there is a whole new world that the student is trying to step into. That is the desired reality. In our desired reality lies all the good things that we are now asking for, whereas these things may be absent or in an undesired state in our current reality. The science of manifestation is thus about stepping into our desired realities as quickly as possible, and with as little fuss or difficulty as possible.

The intent of all my books has been to show readers quick and easy ways to make this transition. When you become a master at deliberate manifestations, you will find that desired changes happen in your life very quickly—sometimes in the blink of an eye. You will find yourself stepping into your desired reality quickly and spontaneously, such that any intentions held quickly become manifest in your outer, physical reality. However, if you are *not* a master at deliberate manifestations, you will find the manifestation process to be slow and arduous. You will find yourself asking a lot and getting desperate, but things will just seem to remain the same for you. This is because you may still be under the influence of past beliefs and past negative conditioning.

Before I became a conscious manifestor, I erroneously thought that the way to get whatever I wanted in life was to "strive" and "work hard" for it. Hence I saw physical action and effort as the only way out. This is the way in which society has taught and conditioned us over hundreds of years. "If you want something, work for it!" is the adage that is constantly being promulgated. This saying works to a certain extent in our physical society, until we realize that there are things that elude us even with our best efforts. There is only *so much* we can do and *so much* physical effort that we can make. In other words, there is a limit as to how much we can physically do before we reach the point of exhaustion.

The easier (and more counterintuitive way) is to do the inner work necessary using our inner focus. Notice how this contrasts with the earlier approach. When we attempt to use our physical strength and physical efforts, we do the outer work that we think has to be done. We attempt to go out into the world and change the conditions out there to suit us. However, when we do the inner work necessary, we do none of that. Instead, we quiet our minds and go into the calmness and peace within. We clear away all blocks on the inside (negative thoughts, emotions, beliefs and feelings) that prevent us from getting what we want. We become *very still* and *very clear* on what it is that we want.

The most amazing thing happens when we reach that state of inner clarity. The first thing that often happens is that outer circumstances now start to rearrange themselves to suit us! Instead of us having to go out there and rearrange things in the world through physical action and effort, now the outer conditions rearrange themselves to suit our intentions. It is as if the whole world is conspiring on our behalf! Opportunities present themselves, people start approaching us and things start falling into place. However, I estimate that less than 5% of the population adopts this way of operating in the world because of a few reasons. First, it requires an extraordinary amount of faith and courage (at least in the beginning). Second, it requires that we do the inner work necessary and channel our inner focus in the right way. And finally, third, it runs contrary to everything that we have been taught in school—and everything that we have been taught about "hard work."

I can write books to convince you about the process and why this should be the way, but there is no substitute for your own personal experience and your own willingness to give this a try. You must be willing to give up everything you know and **try living this way for yourself.** One of my books "Dollars Flow

To Me Easily" talks about the inner path to manifesting money and is all about clearing up the blocks on the inside that prevent abundance from flowing to you. The premise is simple—when you clear up the blocks on the inside, the issues holding you back resolve themselves spontaneously in the outer world. And because abundance is your natural birthright, the dollars have to start flowing to you!

I discovered and finally put myself on that inner path out of desperation. I had tried everything possible in the outer world—including working hard, working smart, saving smart, saving hard (that was a chore), investing smart, getting a good education, coming up with good ideas—quite possibly every single money-making and money-management technique that was known to mankind and was still not going anywhere. Each time I made some progress, something would happen to take that money away. I worried and constantly struggled with money all the time. None of the books I read or techniques I learned over the years seemed to help. Finally, I reasoned that if the answers weren't to be found outside of me, they should all be within me instead.

I am sharing this story here because the same principles apply when learning how to consciously and deliberately manifest your greater good. This is not a process of stamp collection where you amass a toolbox of manifestation techniques that you can then apply to the situation. Far too many spiritual seekers take this Band-Aid approach to spirituality, which may explain why they are *still* seeking! If you wish to be an effective manifestor and conscious creator, you must change the fundamental way that you live and operate. Instead of living in an outer-directed manner where you try to "fix" things on the outside in a piecemeal way (using either physical effort or metaphysical techniques), you have to turn inward and take a good look at what is happening on the inside.

Do you secretly believe in hard work? Do you secretly believe that you cannot have whatever you ask for? Do you believe that things are not going to come easy without a bit of struggle or hard work? All of these beliefs are not "wrong," for whatever we believe and expect often comes true for us. Rather, these are unresourceful and unnecessary beliefs to hold, beliefs that can make the process more convoluted and difficult than it actually is.

Manifestations are easy. They are your natural birthright! We manifest new people, events, physical objects and situations in our lives all the time without much conscious thought and focus. Notice how people, things and events just seem to come and go in your life and become aware that you have a part to play in attracting all of them in some way. Start with this gentle understanding and awareness that you are already a manifestor and creator of everything that is in your life, although not everything pleases you at the moment. This conscious awareness will make it much easier for you to proceed with the rest of the lessons in this book.

The difference between an effective manifestor and a struggling manifestor lies in your choice of focus. In other words, *where* you choose to place your thought energy and what you choose to pay attention to makes all the difference to your outer results.

Effective manifestors are able to place their mental focus singularly on their desired outcomes (even in the face of contrary physical evidence or unpleasant physical symptoms), while struggling manifestors are constantly swayed by physical evidence and by how things currently are in the real world. They are constantly being taken in by the evidence presented by their five senses, not realizing that this "reality" is malleable and can be changed at any time. Struggling manifestors do not realize that the moment they withdraw their physical focus and place no (or less) attention on their undesired realities that the undesired realities start to fade away by themselves without their physical intervention. This is perhaps the most difficult principle to grasp in the whole of these manifestation teachings. The act of turning our focus away from the current reality has been mislabeled by our society as being "impractical," "lazy" or "running away from reality." But as Abraham-Hicks put it, you should never face reality unless it pleases you!

In the beginning, my reality did not really please me. There were many elements of the world I was living in that upset me, that I fervently wanted to change. However, I did not understand that I had a hand in creating *all* of them, even those elements that I did not like! By allowing myself to dwell on these unpleasant aspects of my reality, I was in fact perpetuating my unwanted reality even more.

The second phase of my transformation occurred when I took Abraham-Hicks' advice to heart. Recall in the previous chapter that for years, Abraham-Hicks have been talking about the importance of "telling a new story." What I was doing all along was telling the *old*, worn-out story over and over again while secretly wishing that things could be somewhat different. Of course they could not change! Universal Law always gives you more of what you choose to place your conscious focus on. But one day, after applying an early version of the Magic Transformation process, I decided to *try* telling a new story just for once—and I never looked back.

Telling a new story is perhaps the most unnatural and difficult thing to do in the world, at least in the beginning! If everyone understood how unnatural it feels in the beginning, perhaps it would encourage more people to keep at the process and not deviate from it. When you first start "telling a new story" while still living in your existing reality, it <u>does</u> feel like you're telling a lie. It does feel like you are engaged in wishful thinking, or that you are somehow escaping from your problems. All of these thoughts will flood your mind, and you will have moments where you think to yourself, "Am I losing my mind following this path?"

However, understand that all this is a natural response because your reasoning, rational ego mind has been programmed to keep you safe. Although the current reality may be somewhat unpleasant, it is the *only* reality that you know, and hence it represents something safe and familiar to you. "At least you are safe here" is the unconscious reasoning that most people often hold on to. Therefore, when you first begin to "tell a new story" and to signal your desire for change, the first backlash will come from your conscious reasoning faculties. They are going to give you lots of seemingly "valid" reasons *why* the change you seek is not for your own benefit.

But if you persist at "telling the new story" for long enough (and the time frame varies from one individual to the next), what you'll soon find will be spots and patches of evidence in your outer reality that things have indeed changed. It may be a chance encounter here, a book recommendation there, an observation of certain phenomenon or certain feelings and insights that come to you. The moment you start telling a new story, the Universe reciprocates and the old reality has to fall away.

Therefore, think of all this as a three-part act. The first part is where you live in a current reality where not everything pleases you. How you got to that current reality is not important, but you are there. The second part is where you're trying to bridge the worlds between your current and desired reality. This is the part where you start telling a new story. It is the part that is the most difficult because you have to keep telling the new story *despite* evidence to the contrary. And finally, the third part is where you step fully into your new reality, where the old reality seems so remote and foreign to you even though it may have just been a few short months or years ago. Once you understand this basic structure of manifestation and change, you'll always know where you are along the way.

Chapter Four

Understanding the 3 Manifestation Phases

The three-part manifestation process that I shared in the last chapter is a useful way of "visualizing" where you are along the process. In the beginning, it will take some time to go through the three phases. For example, you may find yourself in the second phase for a few weeks or months as things start to change around you. But as you become more proficient with the process of change and manifestation, you'll find that virtually no time is needed to traverse the three phases. They can happen for you spontaneously—just like that!

It helps to think of any perceived problem or issue in your life right now in terms of the three phases. Doing so will save you from lots of unwanted struggle and negative emotions. For example, if you are currently confronting an undesired situation in your life, ask yourself whether you are in Phase 1, 2 or 3 of the process. Are you currently in Phase 1, where you are complaining and busy rationalizing why things *should not* be the way they are? Or are you in Phase 2, where you are slowly starting to withdraw your attention from the unwanted and focus on the wanted? I can assure you that each time manifestations are slow in coming, it is because you are still spending most of your time in Phase 1 of the process. This is important: You cannot spend most of your time in Phase 1 while expecting things to change for you. This is Universal Law. In other words, you cannot spend the majority of your time sharing your miseries and complaining to others *while expecting* that things will improve for you. That's how powerful you are!

If you are currently in Phase 2 of the process, then rest assured that changes will happen to you very soon. Most people who think they're in Phase 2 are not really in Phase 2 all the time. A closer examination of their thoughts and inner states will reveal that they sometimes slip back into Phase 1 thinking. The more they flip back and forth between these two states, the slower their progress will be. That's because they will be moving in the desired direction, and then moving back in the opposite direction again. I will share more techniques and methods to remain in Phase 2 for most of the time.

Eventually, outer reality changes so much for you that you emerge into Phase 3. Just as it was difficult to imagine a desired reality when the physical signs around you were to the contrary, it is now difficult to imagine an undesired reality when the physical evidence around you pleases you greatly. That's why there is built-in momentum in the manifestation process. When you have been in Phase 2 for quite some time, the little physical changes that occur on the outside often add up, and you find yourself getting swept up by the positive changes that occur. Know that there is momentum and a Universal flow that are assisting you in all of this. If you only do your job of remaining in Phase 2 of the process, then the Universal flow is going to make things progressively easier for you. Similarly, if you allow yourself to be caught up in Phase 1 of the process, the Universal flow is going to make things more and more difficult for you by continuing to present you with more things that upset you.

Now that you understand the three phases of manifestation and creation, let's talk about the time element in all of this. How long do the three phases need to play out? How much time does it take for you to go through the three phases? Or more directly, how much time does it take before what you want manifests for you? The answer may both shock and delight you: Time is irrelevant for manifestations. I explained in my book "Playing in Time and Space" that time is largely an illusion in our space-time Universe and that we use time to make sense of things on a linear scale. When explaining the three phases of the manifestation process, we often add time to the process to "make sense" of things, to tell ourselves that Phase 1 comes before Phase 2, which comes before Phase 3. It is a method our logical minds use to wrap our heads around the process.

Let's try a fun experiment for now. First, ask yourself how long you would expect to take to move from Phase 1 to 3 of the process. In other words, how long does it take (on average) for a manifestation to come true for you? Any number that you come up with will be based on your own personal expectations or your past experiences. We are not looking for an accurate number here, just a figure to work with. So let any number that comes up for you be alright. Let's suppose that the time frame that you have come up with is "a few months." This means that in order to make sense of the manifestation process, your logical thinking brain has ascribed the time frame of "a few months" to the manifestation process.

When I first started my manifestation journey, I too used to believe that the process would take a few weeks to months. That was my logical way of analyzing and interpreting the flow of things. However, a few events quickly changed my understanding about the matter. The first was hearing Abraham-Hicks speak about how spontaneous and instant manifestations are possible in terms of the cells of our bodies. Abraham-Hicks explained that our bodily systems are so advanced that minor corrections and interventions are made almost every single second without our conscious awareness. In other words, the problem is solved before we even have a conscious awareness that there was a problem in the first place! The more I thought about it, the more I realized how true this is. Our bodily systems are constantly fighting and neutralizing antigens, stabilizing our various bodily processes without our active intervention. There is an innate intelligence that takes care of all this. More importantly, this innate intelligence *corrects the situation* even before we recognize there is a problem.

This is an important piece in our understanding of the three-phase manifestation process and how it relates to the passage of time. If we see Phase 1 as our conscious recognition of the issue (or undesired situation that we want to change) and our time spent focusing on the undesired reality, Phase 2 as focusing on the desired reality and Phase 3 as stepping into our desired reality, then what Abraham-Hicks are teaching is that Phases 1 and 2 can happen so quickly and unconsciously that we jump straight to Phase 3 at once! That's not some far-fetched theory. In fact, it is happening right now with the cells and organs in our bodies.

Another example that Abraham-Hicks gave was driving on our roads. Drivers will know what I am talking about here. Have you ever had a hunch that the other driver was about to do something funny and swerved or braked just in time to avoid an accident? That is yet another example of applying a very fast corrective action. You jumped from Phase 2 to Phase 3 immediately, bypassing the undesired reality in Phase 1.

These examples, along with new manifestation modalities and teachings in our world right now, suggest that the manifestation timeline is more malleable than perceived. Some of the healing modalities that contribute to this change in consciousness include Emotional Freedom Techniques (EFT or tapping), Matrix Energetics, the Yuen Method and so on. All of these healing modalities teach that change happens in an *instant.* (By the way, you can pick up all of these healing modalities much more easily when you apply the Magic Transformation to them.) I have experienced this to be true for myself, and have obtained instant results through all of these modalities. The greater significance of all this is that no time is needed at all for Phase 2 to take place. Change can happen in the blink of an eye. The shift in Phase 2 can happen so instantaneously that we do not even perceive the change process consciously, and yet change has occurred. This is the idea of spontaneity that I'm trying to convey in this book.

Take the amount of time that you stated earlier (it may be a few days, weeks or months) and just *imagine* that time being compressed into a few seconds, or less than a second. Observe how that feels for you. See yourself going through Phases 1, 2 and 3 of the manifestation process in a few seconds instead of a few months. How does that feel for you? Does the possibility excite and energize you? After all, if manifestations can stretch out and take seemingly *forever* to happen for some people (a few months to years), then why can't that time be compressed in the *opposite* direction? Why can't we compress those few months or years required into just a few seconds, or less than a second? All this is possible once you understand the illusory nature of time and how to work with it. Feel this sense of possibility in your body.

And while you may still not fully believe that manifestations (the process of change) can be spontaneous, just entertain the possibility of how this would be if it were true for you. Remember what we discussed in the opening chapter? People often perpetuate their existing unwanted realities by *refusing* to even consider the possibilities. When you entertain the thoughts of an alternative reality in your own mind, you are doing more than just using your imagination or "playing a mind game." You are taking the very important step of moving toward Phase 2 of the process. You soften your focus on the undesired reality and place that focus on a possibility that is more desired. This is the catalyst and seed necessary for all manifestations to take place.

As we round up this chapter, I would like you to apply the two principles you have learned in your own life. First, identify an issue that has been long-standing for you. This may be something that has bothered you for quite some time. Ask yourself whether you are currently in Phase 1 or 2 of the manifestation process. You'll find that each time you struggle with manifesting something, it is always because you are spending more time in Phase 1 than in Phase 2. Just bring your gentle awareness to this observation without trying to change any of it.

Next, remind yourself that the process of change can be instantaneous. You can go to sleep one night and then wake up the next morning to a whole new reality, if that is what you have intended. None of that struggling or gradual change process is necessary. Right now, just contemplate the possibility that change can be instantaneous for you, and for this particular issue in your life that you have chosen to place your focus on. Know that this situation, as with all current reality, is temporary and malleable. Know that the situation is not cast in stone and can be changed at any time. Once the energy beneath the situation shifts, then existing reality has to collapse and give way to an alternative, more welcome reality.

For now, ponder this possibility in your mind and *feel* how you would feel if change happened in an instant for you. How would you feel if you stepped into your new reality in just a few seconds? These feelings go beyond wishful daydreaming or your imagination. They give you a very real taste of what things are like in that alternative and more desired reality in Phase 3. These are the actual feelings you'll tap into when you are in that more desired reality, and you have access to them right now. The more you bring up and ponder what these desired feelings feel like to you, the more time you'll spend in your desired reality, which means that your existing reality has to start fading away.

Chapter Five
The Quick Statement Process

Let's review our discussion so far. First, we established that there are three stages to the manifestation process. And that as long as you allow yourself to be stuck in Phase 1, you will find it difficult to make any meaningful progress in terms of your outer reality. We also learned that once you allow yourself to move into Phase 2 and stay there for most of the time (despite contrary physical evidence), then the momentum of the Universal flow is going to carry you along. The Law of Attraction is going to attract more like thoughts, feelings and experiences, which will make it progressively easier for you to stay in Phase 2 and focus on what you want.

But perhaps the most important insight we discussed is that the time you spend in Phase 2 can be compressed to under a second. It can happen so quickly, even instantaneously that you do not have any conscious awareness that any time has passed. We know this to be possible not only from the teachings of the great spiritual masters, but also from new healing modalities that are emerging and developing on our planet this very moment. As human consciousness evolves, we begin to transcend the conventional time and space limitations and explore tools that will lead to instant change. This is the framework that we will be building on for the rest of this book.

In this chapter, I would like to talk about moving past the manifestation blocks that hold you back in Phase 1. Recall that as long as you *remain* in Phase 1 and continue to place your focus on unwanted reality, then things will have a difficult time changing for you. This is in accordance with Universal Law and you can prove it to yourself very easily by taking a look at the things that are happening in your own life. All the things that you have spent huge amounts of time and energy complaining about are still there in your life. They are the most stubborn of phenomena, simply refusing to yield to any form of corrective action!

Yet this point is also the most difficult to get because we often get caught up in a chicken-and-egg situation. Some people may say, "Well, the reason why I spend so much time talking about it is because the problem is difficult to get rid of! It's a serious issue!" Notice what has just happened here. They have just confused the consequence (the seriousness or persistence of the issue) with the cause (their continued focus on it). Most people do not realize that the issue is persistent in their reality *precisely because* of their continued focus on it. When they place that focus elsewhere, they no longer feed any thought energy into the situation and whatever problem or issue they perceive has to fall apart.

Most of my books are about persuading my readers to soften their focus on the undesirable issues in their lives. I know that if I can get them to soften their focus on the undesirable aspects of their lives for even one moment, then the Universe can step in to do its magic. I am heartened to know that many readers have taken these teachings to heart and tried these techniques for themselves, obtaining great results in the process. There is no way I can physically *do it* for you, as the inner work always has to be done by yourself. But I can share my own experiences and tell you how I managed to do it. Hopefully, you'll be able to glean some useful points from learning about my experience.

The core of Abraham-Hicks' teachings is the importance of telling a new story. What this means is placing absolutely no focus on the undesired aspects of our reality. As I mentioned earlier, while this is easy to advocate from a non-physical perspective, it is extremely difficult to put into practice from a physical perspective. Our five senses dominate our everyday experiences so much that we find it so difficult to ignore the constant input from our senses. Yet once I applied the Magic Transformation on the teachings of Abraham-Hicks, I saw that this is precisely what Abraham-Hicks have been telling us to do: Place absolutely no focus on your undesired reality, and <u>all your focus</u> on your desired reality.

When you do so, you will step into your desired reality quickly.

If the whole science of manifestations can be summarized into one single sentence, then why is it that so many people have trouble doing it? Why is it that so many people out there are still struggling with their manifestations, to the point of asserting that these manifestation principles do not work? I have found that the answer is simple. We place too much emphasis on what comes through our five senses and we believe too much in the persistence of the current reality. We believe that things are set in stone and are unlikely to change. This applies even for me, someone who has done much inner work and written about this Universal Law. Therefore, we must develop a conscious moment-to-moment awareness that everything is just energy, and can shift just as easily with our intentions.

I would like to offer a process that can make things easier for you and aid in the transition from Phase 1 to 2 of the manifestation process. I call this the Quick Statement process and have found it to be useful for getting to the core of any matter and dropping any negative blocks that hold me back.

Those who have read my other books will know that I do not advocate dwelling on any unwanted issue in our lives for a protracted period of time. There is very little value in psychoanalyzing the causes and sources of our problems because such analysis is usually unreliable and tainted by our unconscious beliefs, expectations and past experiences in life. For example, some people may say, "I am poor this life because I made a poverty vow in one of my previous lives." Or "I am overweight in this life because I had very little to eat in my previous life." Now this may or may not be true, but once our conscious minds have locked on to a particular line of reasoning, they start developing a story around this belief that will make it seem true for us. We begin to pick up (or conjure) more evidence that is consistent with this belief, until we finally have a whole host of real and imagined beliefs to deal with. In other words, we get deeper and deeper into the story, when the whole point is to be free from any story in the first place.

Recall that the point of all these teachings is to be free from the influence of our beliefs and negative feelings. Therefore, there is very little value in dwelling on the causes and sources of the unwanted issues in our lives. Let's suppose that you are dealing with an unpleasant colleague at work. There is little value in psychoanalyzing the causes of his unpleasant behavior and trying to figure out why he is acting the way he does. You may come up with some very clever and seemingly valid scientific explanations (as I used to do), and they may seem *true* for you, but you'll soon realize at the end of the day that these explanations (while seemingly valid) do absolutely nothing to correct the situation! They are also almost always wrong because whatever reasons we come up with are tainted by our own personal experiences and beliefs.

The same occurs in the area of family relationship issues. The good news is that there is no need to spend an inordinate amount of time trying to figure out *why* someone is acting in a particular way or what is upsetting him or her. This form of psychoanalysis just causes us to be trapped in Phase 1 for a longer time than necessary. In the words of Abraham-Hicks, the sole purpose of any unpleasant, undesired situation in our lives is to catapult us to a more desired reality. This "contrast" (between what we desire and what is currently in our reality) serves the useful purpose of helping us identify what we want, and nothing more. There is no value in dwelling in the "contrast" for a longer period than necessary.

Let's apply this to the area of manifesting physical items in your life. Suppose that you have been trying to manifest a particular item for a long time and the lack of results is causing you considerable frustration and disappointment. You ask the earlier question of whether you are in Phase 1 or 2 and find that you are still dwelling in Phase 1 most of the time—you constantly talk about your undesired reality, worry over how you will get what you want, become frustrated over the results and so on. To make things worse, there are certain physical triggers in your outer reality that upset you even further. For example, let's suppose that your intention is to manifest a new car to replace your old one that frequently breaks down and is in need of repairs. The condition of your current car is particularly obvious and sticks out like a sore thumb for you because you most likely depend on it on a daily basis. All of this can lead to feelings of frustration, helplessness and disappointment, as if there is no way out of your current situation.

The good news is that all these negative emotions surrounding your current situation are causing the supposed manifestation delay. You may attribute your "lack of manifestation" to the lack of available funds to purchase the new car, but let me assure you that the reasons or blocks you perceive are rarely what they are. This is perhaps the greatest news in all of these teachings! That's why I do not advocate dwelling on the source of your problems or supposed blockages. Very often, the limitations and blockages that we perceive are not "actual" limitations at all! They do not even matter to the Universe.

As counterintuitive as it may sound, the cause of your delayed manifestations is always the negative emotions that you hold regarding the matter. Once you realize this, you'll understand why clearing up all of the negative emotions that you hold surrounding an intention makes it happen very quickly in your reality. This is Universal Law and the nature of our Universe!

Now that we know *how* to do it, why don't more of us put it into action? The truth is already laid out, plain and simple, in front of us, yet why do we still hold on to all our negative feelings surrounding our manifestations or a particular situation? The answer is simple. As physical beings, we experience a lot of inertia and inner resistance that prevent us from dropping our negative feelings quickly. Many of us will even go as far to assert that there is no way we can be free from our negative feelings because we are so immersed in them!

No matter what negative feelings you hold right now regarding any situation, know that there is a fast and effective way that you can let them go. I call this the Quick Statement process and it is based on the teachings of Abraham-Hicks. I find the Quick Statement process to be especially useful when I am caught up in the heat of the moment, when I am overwhelmed by those negative feelings of fear, worry or frustration. I use it whenever I feel that there is nothing I can do to change the situation.

The beautiful thing about the Quick Statement process is that it does not require you to analyze the situation or break down the problem. It cuts right through to what matters and helps you dissolve the negative emotions surrounding any situation quickly and easily. The way to apply the Quick Statement process is simple. Whenever you are feeling immense negative emotions, <u>stop</u> for a moment and ask yourself: What is it that I want in this situation?

Let the answers come to you naturally. You'll often find the answer bubbling from the depths of your consciousness. For example, suppose that you are embroiled in a tumultous family relationship. Everything your partner says irritates you and you feel yourself entertaining violent thoughts about the situation. In that moment, there would be immense value for you to stop and ask (even out loud to yourself): "What is it that I want in this situation?" You'll find the answers coming forth spontaneously with great clarity, for it is situations like this that cause you to ask with great intensity. "I want peace. I want a joyous relationship with my partner" may be the answer that you receive.

Take a close look at the answer because it will show you a tangible path to get to Phase 2 of the manifestation process. Whatever you have just answered is **what you should focus on wholeheartedly.** Put differently, if you focus on what is it that you want (as stated in the answer that you gave), then you are cutting through all of the negative emotions and getting to Phase 2 of the manifestation process immediately, without any fuss or struggle.

Don't let the apparent simplicity of this technique fool you. I often found myself embroiled in unhappiness and negative emotions for a few days before remembering to use this technique! When I asked myself the question, "What is it that I want in this situation?" the answers usually came forth from my inner being loud and clear. In each case, all of the negativity and bad feelings (often about the other party) fell away as I realized it was my job to focus solely on whatever I wanted, not on the other party or my negative feelings.

In the case of manifesting a new car, your answer may be: "I want my new car to come to me easily." That answer, while deceptively simple, is actually an aha moment for you. Once again, the answers that your inner being gives may be different from what I am suggesting here, but they will always be just right for you. Whatever answers you get will be tailored exactly to your situation and circumstances. You have been worried and frustrated about the slow manifestation of your new car and suddenly receive the clarity that you need to move forward with the process. You realize that instead of dwelling on all the negative feelings of worry and frustration, all you need to do is to dwell single-pointedly on the feelings of "ease." Therefore, the Quick Statement process actually helps you by formulating a single statement (again, keep it to a few words) that states your highest intention clearly and succinctly.

Try the Quick Statement process for yourself right now. I have found that the process works even better in the midst of intense negative emotions because that is when we are asking the hardest questions and summoning forth Universal energies with great intensity. But try the Quick Statement process in any situation. You may be surprised at the simplicity and profoundness of the answers that you receive, as I always have. Remember—the objective of the Quick Statement process is not to rationalize or think logically about what you want. It is to create an opening that allows your inner being to speak and reveal its true feelings about the situation. Sometimes, the answers you get may be as succinct as: "I want peace."

This is your inner being's way of telling you that its highest intention for the situation is peace and nothing else. This is the answer that is the most authentic, which you most need to hear at that point in time. If you only focus on this feeling of peace to the exclusion of everything else, you'll find the outer manifestations happening very quickly for you.

Chapter Six

The Universe Always Supports You!

I would like to share a few amazing manifestations that unfolded as a result of using the Quick Statement process. The first happened more than ten years ago when I was still actively running one of my businesses. I had become so caught up in the daily grind—negotiating with customers and suppliers, trying to market for new business, setting up appointments, managing staff—that I became very discouraged and frustrated by it all. The level of success that I envisioned for my business seemed so far away despite all the physical effort and hard work I put into it. The long hours and constant stress from thinking about what I was going to do next and how I was going to reach my goals was wearing me down. I had such a beautiful vision for my business on paper, so why wasn't any of it translating into reality? Why did it seem so difficult when the proverbial rubber finally met the road?

One day, out of sheer desperation, I decided to use an early version of the Quick Statement process.

I sat myself down amid all the frenzy and asked: What is it that I really want from my business?

Instantly, the unexpected answer came through loud and clear: "I want to make money from this venture." That was an audacious response that shocked me because up until that point, I had consciously denied that I was going into business for the money. When asked, I tried to use all kinds of excuses to *mask* the fact that I was in it for the money, from convincing myself (and others) that I was in it for the experience to telling myself that my business venture would enrich the lives of my customers. Little did I realize that those were simply rationalizations by my conscious mind. What I really wanted so badly from the venture was to make money from it.

Now this may seem like a mercenary reason for getting into business, but the answer you get when you use the Quick Statement process is always the most authentic and reveals your highest intentions, whatever they may be. You simply cannot lie when you use the Quick Statement process as your highest intentions are always revealed to you when you take the time to ask. It took me only a split second to realize that the response was right. Back then, I still had not embarked on this spiritual journey nor delved into a deep study of all this metaphysical material, but I knew that the answer held the key to what I was looking for.

I felt unfulfilled because I went into business intending to make money, and yet here I was, not making any money from this venture. This was the real reason behind my deep dissatisfaction. By refusing to acknowledge my actual intentions for starting my business, I was only driving myself further into unhappiness.

As you use the Quick Statement process at different points and on different situations in your life, you'll find the answers constantly evolving. That is to be expected because the Quick Statement process is meant to reveal your highest intentions without any rationalizations or logical reasoning. It is meant to be a process where you can quickly gather key insights (the truths) about the situation and move past your blocks instead of dwelling on them. Therefore, do not judge whatever answers come up for you from the Quick Statement process. The intention of using the Quick Statement process is just that—to come up with a Quick Statement that accurately summarizes what you want.

When I realized that my intention for the business was to make money, I began examining what I was doing on a daily basis. It became apparent to me that I was being pulled in so many different directions! Instead of placing my focus on profits, I had tried to become so many different things at once to different people. I unknowingly used the business as my vehicle to try to become famous, to try to impress others, to build better relationships and so on. The direction that I was taking my business in on a daily basis was moving me further and further away from my original intention. That was the cause of my distress and dissatisfaction.

The Quick Statement that I derived from this method helped me focus on my desired reality. I immediately went back to work with a new mindset. No more trying to please everyone. No more trying to position myself as an expert in my field. No more trying to run my business as a charity. Instead, I focused on my original, honest intention of "making money." When you allow yourself to fulfill your original intention, then all the corollary intentions come true for you as well. Everything else becomes well taken care of.

Did it work? Within two weeks of applying the Quick Statement process and with a mere refocusing of my energy, I landed a new client who subsequently became a business partner I worked closely with over the next few years. The partnership made us six figures in less than a year—the most money I had ever made in my life at that point! In fact, the client initially hired me for a sum of five figures, also the most I had charged at that point! The most amazing thing about this new client was that I did not approach her. She contacted me out of the blue within two weeks after I did the Quick Statement process. She was also a dream client, willing to pay whatever price I asked and never once haggled over my fees.

Nothing changed on the outside. I did not engage in any deliberate actions to bring about more business. A mere shift in my inner state was all that was necessary to bring about this new business partner in my life. I realize now that I was tapping on these exact same manifestation principles that I actively teach today. If I had become conscious of these principles sooner, I could have sidestepped much of the struggle and learning curve.

The greatest lesson that came out from this episode is that the Universe *always* supports you in your endeavors, whatever they may be. The Universe (life itself) always gives you what you want, if you have the courage to claim it. As spiritual teacher and founder of the Unity movement Charles Fillmore puts it, "It is the Father's good pleasure to give us the kingdom, and all that the Father has is ours. But we must have the faith and the courage to claim it." Therefore, do not be afraid to ask boldly for what you want. Do not be like the person I was, to ask and then not have the courage to claim what I asked for out of fear. Looking back, I can see why I behaved in that way. I had many fears and concerns, primarily the fear of being judged by others: "What would others think of me if they knew what I was asking for?" As I have come to realize, freeing myself from the judgments of others is the ultimate freedom. (Read my book "Today I Am Free" for more.)

I continued to run the business for a few more years, making good money from it, until I noticed the familiar feelings of dissatisfaction and stress start to surface. So I used the Quick Statement process again: "What do I want from this business?" This time, the answer was completely different from what I received previously. "I want joy from this business." As you can see, I moved from wanting to make money to wanting joy from the business. My intentions had shifted. I no longer wanted to make money from the venture. I had fulfilled that earlier intention. Although I was making good money from the work, the business no longer aligned with the new intentions for the next stage of my life. I could see that my dissatisfaction stemmed from the discrepancy between what I wanted (joy) and what I was getting from my business (only money, but very little joy). With this realization, I decided to give up my business and move on to something else. The "moving on" process became very easy and effortless, much to the surprise of my clients!

We often find ourselves hesitant to give up something that we have built over a long period of time. Conventional wisdom tells us that abandoning something that we took a long time to build is silly and a waste of our prior efforts. But as students of these metaphysical principles, we know that "hard work" is never part of the equation. Therefore, there can never be any "wasted time" or "wasted effort" in building up anything. If we want to, we can just as easily flourish in our new endeavors within a very short time as we did in the old ones. Time is irrelevant in the entire equation. Alignment between our inner states and highest intentions is what matters.

Others in my position would have been reluctant to give up their old businesses, having spent so much time building them up. They would have been reluctant to give up their reputations, existing customers or comfortable income streams. But there would have been very little joy left in staying in my old business. My old business venture was just a vehicle that I used to fulfill my intention of making money at that point in my life. Once that intention was fulfilled and the lessons learned, the vehicle had served its purpose. I am now on the lookout for new vehicles and new ways to fulfill my higher purpose.

The good news in all of this is that you do not have to worry about what your new vehicle will be. You never have to worry about the means through which your new intentions will be fulfilled. The Universe always gives you a clue and points you in the right direction, if only you're willing to listen. Let the Universe unfold the next step for you. Writing these series of books serves as a new vehicle for me now, and it gives me so much joy just to write and share my ideas with readers from all over the world. I write directly from my heart, never once censoring my thoughts, feelings or ideas because this is the new direction that the Universe has pointed me in. I no longer make the earlier mistake of being afraid to claim what I have asked for. When you do whatever that makes your heart sing, you participate *in* the Universal Flow and honor your highest intentions. This would not have been possible for me had I stubbornly held on to my old business venture just "for the money."

Take a look at your own life. What clues has the Universe dropped along the way for you? What dissatisfaction or discontent have you recently felt regarding certain areas of your life? Instead of resenting these feelings for what they are, apply the Quick Statement process to get at the underlying nudges. They may open the door to more fulfilling manifestations in your life. I would never have imagined becoming a ten-time best-selling author, especially without the support of a major publishing house and in this fiercely competitive industry. But I did it because I was *in* the Universal Flow. I had the backing of the Universe. You, too have the backing of the Universe in whatever you do. Enlist it as your business partner and your marketing manager. It all starts with placing your focus on what you want and then having the courage to claim it on the inside. When you awaken to your power and potential on the inside, that is when all the manifestations and good things start happening on the outside—but you must have the faith and courage to claim it!

Chapter Seven

Identifying Intimate Manifestation Touchstones Just For You

The ability to notice what is different is a crucial skill in the manifestation process. After you have applied the Quick Statement process and identified your highest intention in any situation, the next step is to sit back and quietly notice the subtle differences that take place in your reality. Bear in mind that the manifestation process is not one to be rushed or forced. The timing of your manifestations is not up to you. Neither are the ways through which your manifestations will come under your control. Seeking to control these two elements of the manifestation process (the timing and means) can only mean unnecessary headache and struggle. They are not your work to begin with!

Very often, simply coming up with a Quick Statement such as "I want joy" will clear up much of the negative feelings and emotions surrounding the situation. You'll find much of your extraneous negative emotions melting away, as they did for me when I realized that I was allowing my attention to be dictated by insignificant concerns. When I realized that I wasn't in business to please everyone, to become famous or to help everyone that came my way, all the mental anguish and emotions from dealing with clients and suppliers vanished. In their place was a sense of purpose and clarity. "I know what my highest intentions are for this situation and I am acting in accordance to them." This is why the Quick Statement process is so valuable yet deceptively simple. Instead of rationalizing through all the negative feelings that are clouding your perception, the identification of a single quick statement is all it takes to shift your focus (and energies) about any situation. Remember that whatever you place your focus on is where the energy flows. And where the energy flows for most of the time gives you a clue as to what is going to manifest.

You'll find that the Quick Statement process helps you to step into Phase 2 of the manifestation process more easily. Use the Quick Statement as a guide, a doorway to help you get into Phase 2. That's what it is—a single, succinct statement that accurately captures your highest intentions and feelings associated with your desired reality. It is recommended that you come up with a short statement representing whatever you wish to manifest in life. You do so not to "state your intentions clearly to the Universe," but rather, to state your intentions clearly to yourself. I have found that spontaneous shifts happened whenever I could find the right representing statement to accurately sum up my feelings and intentions. Let me illustrate this with a few examples.

We often think that describing the item we want is the best way of stating our intentions. For example, if you are looking for a classic watch with a brown leather strap, you may intend: "I intend a classic watch with a brown leather strap." But that is nothing more than a plain description of the item that fails to evoke any of the relevant emotions and feelings in you. How will you feel when you are in Phase 2 or even Phase 3 of the process? How will you feel when you are finally in that desired reality, where you have that watch with a brown leather strap sitting on your wrist? How will you feel when you wear that watch as you go about your daily activities? The first statement that you have come up with cannot answer any of these questions and hence is not an effective doorway to your manifestations. Remember that your intention here is to come up with a Quick Statement that sums up all the desired feelings that come from the eventual manifestation.

So let's see if we can spruce up the original statement a bit. How about this: "I am wearing a classic watch with a brown leather strap." That's a step in the right direction. Many self-help and spiritual teachers recommend the use of the words "I AM," to signify that you *are* already that which you ask for. This new statement is an improvement over the first one, in that you feel stronger feelings associated with the use of the words "I AM." But can you do better than that?

How about: "I enjoy glancing down at the smooth-polished dial of my Rolex watch as I sit in meetings." *Now* you are getting somewhere. You'll find that this new statement evokes considerably more emotions than the previous two. It is also a statement that is more intimate and applicable to your own unique setting. Perhaps you spend quite a bit of time in meetings and find yourself glancing discreetly at your watch from time to time. How would it feel to look down at the dial of not just any watch, but *your* dream watch? You can even go one step further and state: "I enjoy glancing discreetly at the smooth, polished dial of my Rolex watch in meetings and feeling an immense sense of satisfaction from owning this beautiful watch." Notice the richness of the feelings stirred up by this statement that was not present in the earlier versions. Now you are really getting somewhere!

I would like to take you through another example, this time as applied to the manifestation of a car. You can use this process to manifest anything you like in life, whether tangible or intangible. Simply follow the process and tweak the statements until they evoke highly personal and pleasant feelings just right for you.

Suppose that you would like to manifest a Mercedes-Benz S500 hybrid sedan. Simply stating: "I intend to own and drive a Mercedes-Benz S500 hybrid" doesn't sound terribly exciting. It sounds more like a description of what you want and does not evoke any deep feelings within you. You could just as easily be describing someone else's car. Think of how it would feel if you owned the car this very moment, and if it was parked in your driveway. What emotions would you feel?

"I feel so happy looking out of my window and seeing my black S500 hybrid parked in my driveway." Now this is an improvement over the earlier statement in terms of the feelings associated with your manifestation. Your aim here is to keep reaching for better and better-feeling statements until you cannot go any higher. The more successfully you do so on the inside, the faster your outer manifestations will come about on the outside! Another key is that these better-feeling statements will always be highly personal and applicable only to you. The more narrowly focused the statement is, the better it represents your unique situation.

This is how one might improve on the earlier statement: "I feel so happy driving down Elm Street and smelling the rich leather trim of my S500." Notice that the references to the particular street that you live on (or your favorite stretch in town) will be highly personal for you.

Here are a few other possibilities. Your aim is to move higher and higher up the emotional scale with each improved statement, using your feelings as a gauge.

"I hear my spouse / partner / friend congratulating me as I drive down Elm Street, waving to the neighbors in my new S500."

"I enjoy wrapping my hands around the hand-stitched steering wheel of my S500 while cruising along Elm Street."

"I enjoy calling my wife through the hands-free Bluetooth system in my new S500."

It does not matter which statement you eventually settle on. What matters is that the chosen statement brings about highly intense and pleasant feelings <u>for you</u> that accurately describe the eventual manifestation.

Take as much time as you need for the process. Identifying this unique statement takes time, so do so over the course of the next few days if required. Whenever you have some free time, bring to mind the last statement that you have come up with and see if you can improve it in some way. Then *feel the feelings* associated with the new statement. Is it an improvement in terms of feelings over the previous statement? If so, keep the new statement and work on it further.

Have you ever had a sore spot massaged? Initially, masseurs just poke their fingers around the general area trying to get at the right spot, along with some verbal feedback from you. Finally, after a few rounds of trying, they may hit that exact sore spot, which brings you a great sense of relief! This is the feeling you are going for here, of hunting around for the right words to use that will eventually bring about feelings of *euphoria* and *joy* associated with your final manifestation. The words that you use to get there do not matter. What matters is that you eventually get there in terms of your feelings. When you do so, you will have accessed a very special doorway between your current (Phase 1) and desired reality (Phase 3).

These unique and pleasant feelings serve as manifestation touchstones that you can revisit from time to time. The more time you spend immersed in these feelings, the faster your current reality will shift into your desired reality. In fact, changes will happen right from the very first moment you *feel* your desired reality with absolutely no time lag in between. If you continue to do so with some persistence and focus, you'll see results in your outer reality within a very short time, often in a matter of days.

Over the next few days, quietly notice what is different in your outer reality without attempting to change or influence any of it. Recall, I mentioned at the beginning of this chapter that the "ability to notice" is key to your outer manifestations. You must be able to pick up subtle signs and clues that have emerged in your outer reality. These will lead the way to your eventual manifestations.

In the beginning, the physical signs will be very slight and subtle. You will thus need a keen sense of awareness to pick them up. It is also very easy to dismiss the changes that have occurred as mere coincidences, but resist the urge to do so! You'll be closing your doors to the Universe's guidance if you do so.

Suppose that you try these techniques on your long-standing financial situation. Over the next week, you suddenly receive a few calls inquiring about your services. This is a common scenario whenever my readers apply these manifestation principles in their own lives. They suddenly find business opportunities and people knocking on their doors out of the blue, despite not having changed any of their marketing efforts. However, they quickly become discouraged when the calls do not work out for them. It is this discouragement they allow themselves to feel that moves them quickly back into Phase 1. They were focusing on their desired realities all along *until* they became influenced by an outer, physical sign. Do you now see why you can sometimes slow down the progress of your own manifestations?

Instead of being discouraged by the calls that did not work out, you should realize that the phone has not been ringing for the past few months. And now, after applying these simple manifestation techniques and doing absolutely nothing on the outside, the phones have started ringing again, out of the blue! That is the *clearest* sign from the Universe that you are doing something right! If you just keep focusing on your desired realities and move in this direction, better and bigger things are bound to happen!

The same applies when using this technique on a long-standing health issue. Suppose that after focusing on your desired reality for a while, you find that your symptoms have improved by 10%. Many people will be disappointed that full healing has not occurred and that the improvement has only been slight. However, I often remind them that it is a step in the right direction! If you have been suffering for *years* with absolutely no relief in sight and nothing you tried in the past has ever worked, then this 10% improvement is all the more valuable. You have made overnight progress, when no improvement had been made previously! Of course, it would be good if you could achieve a 90% or even 100% resolution of the situation at once (which is not uncommon), but a 10% resolution on the first try should be welcomed and looked on as a sign of moving in the right direction.

So always be on the lookout for that 5 or 10% improvement in any situation, especially in the beginning. It holds the key to the full manifestation of what is desired.

Chapter Eight

Mastering Non-Linear Manifestations

So far, we have viewed manifestations as a linear creation process, starting with Phase 1 and then moving progressively into Phases 2 and 3 where our final manifestations occur. While viewing the manifestation process in a linear manner allows us to understand the whole process and make sense of things, it is useful to abandon our linear way of thinking and embrace non-linearity as we become more familiar with these Universal principles.

Many of the spiritual healing techniques and modalities that are emerging in the world today emphasize the non-linear nature of the Universe. This means that instead of following a fixed, linear process where healers go through prescribed series of steps one after another, they may move backward and forward in the process, often in a seemingly random fashion. However, you'll realize that there really is a "method to the madness" once you probe deeper. While healers often seem to be doing a bunch of random things at once and jumping from one step to another, you'll understand (once you know the process) that they are really not. They are actually opening themselves up to Universal guidance and letting divine intelligence guide them on what to do next. Because time and space limitations do not matter to the Universe, many of the "next" steps presented by the Universe can seem to be backward or even haphazard in nature. Once you develop an appreciation for this truth, you'll find it easier to take many of the future steps that the Universe prompts you to do. It also becomes much easier to trust that the Universe will deliver whatever you want to you.

For now, picture the three phases of manifestation on a linear timeline, one followed by another. Recall that in an earlier exercise, I asked you to assign an arbitrary time period to the entire timeline. You may have initially ascribed the time of a few weeks or a few months for the entire manifestation process (timeline) to unfold.

Next, I asked you to collapse the time it takes for the entire manifestation process into just a few seconds or under a second. Recall the feelings of exhilaration as you pondered this possibility in your consciousness. You may never have considered this a real possibility before as part of your way of living and operating in this world, but the possibility now exists in your consciousness as a seed that you just planted with this exercise. Just for now, see the whole timeline taking place over the span of one single second (or less), where you move from Phase 1 (identifying what you want) to Phase 3 (the final manifestation) in a very short period of physical time.

Now, let's take things one step further. In your mind's eye, I would like you to collapse the three phases such that they all merge into one. You may find it easier to do this exercise with your eyes closed. First, picture the timeline, stretching out in a linear fashion over the period of three months. Next, compress the whole time period into one second or less. This means that your timeline becomes extremely short and almost a single point / vertical line in your mind's eye. You may then have to zoom in and magnify it a little! Finally, collapse the three distinct phases of the timeline into one single phase. How you visually represent this will be personal and unique for you. For me, I see each of the three phases as three different shaded boxes. When I visualize "collapsing" the three phases into one, I picture the three shaded boxes overlapping, one on top of each other, and occupying the same space all at the same time.

As the last step in this process, picture the single phase (comprising of the three shaded rectangles, one overlapping another) collapsing and compressing itself into a single point or black dot, much like the period at the end of this sentence. If you would like, take a blank sheet of paper and dot a single point in the middle of it. That black dot represents the sum total of your manifestation experiences, all happening in this moment—right now.

What I have just described for you is a visual representation of how our Universe perceives time and space. As I shared in my book "Playing In Time And Space," time is nothing but an illusion. While we perceive time in a linear fashion stretched out into the future, the Universe perceives it as a single black dot all happening right now. Once we understand the illusory nature of time, we can compress or expand time at will and use this to our manifestation advantage, which is another technique I teach in that book. Most readers find it difficult to grasp the notion that time is an illusion, or that everything exists in a single point (in the single now moment). The exercise above makes it easier for them to see the differences between the Universe's point of view and the physical point of view.

With this new understanding, let us take a whole fresh look at the linear manifestation process that we have become so used to.

First, I would like you to bring to mind a case in which your manifestations came easily for you. I can think of many such instances in my life where whatever I wanted just flowed easily into my experience, almost spontaneously and serendipitously as I was going about my daily activities. I would walk right into a store and find the item I want on discount or I would be led along a series of steps where the opportunity to own what I wanted presented itself to me. As you ponder this experience in your own mind, gently *notice* what is different in this experience as compared to a situation where the manifestation was difficult. Remember that the ability to quickly notice any differences is crucial to deliberate manifestations.

You will notice that two things are conspicuously absent whenever manifestations occur easily and effortlessly in your life: First, there is the absence of *worry* and *fear* over whether you will get what you ask for. Second, there is an absence of *time*. Both of these are highly significant keys to understanding spontaneous manifestations, so let's explore each of them in greater detail below.

Each time manifestations happened spontaneously for me, I knew right from the beginning that what I asked for was mine. There was no question and not a single bit of doubt in myself even in the very beginning when the first signs of physical manifestation had not yet occurred! I just knew that whatever I asked for *was already mine* and that an unfolding process just had to occur to bring it to me. Therefore, time was irrelevant or absent in the whole process. I knew it was going to happen and expected it wholeheartedly.

Scenarios like this occur more frequently than you realize in your own life. For example, you *know* that you are going to drink that cup of coffee once you wake up in the morning. Hence the manifestation is settled! You do not worry over *how* you will get it or *whether* it will come to you. Neither do you berate the physical "time" that stands between your current moment and tomorrow morning when you will finally enjoy your cup of coffee. These manifestation principles apply equally to whatever items or states that you ask for in life.

Each time I struggled with manifesting something, I was always tripped up by two major things. First, I allowed myself to feel negative worries and fears regarding the manifestation process. Most of these worries and fears were related to *how* I was going to get something and whether I would get it eventually. Also, I found myself worrying about how much *time* it would take before what I wanted would finally manifest in my experience (Can I manifest it in time?). Negative feelings and worries over time (How long something would take?) are really the two major showstoppers when it comes to physical manifestations!

Suppose that you are currently in Phase 1 of the manifestation process. From your vantage point, Phases 2 and 3 of the process have not played out yet. Those are still indeterminate states in the future in which anything can happen. When you view the manifestation process in such a linear fashion, it is easy to see why concerns about time and worries over the eventual physical manifestation occur. It is because you have limited yourself to a linear perspective of things in which you are trapped at a spot in the "present" and unable to foresee what is happening in the "future"! This uncertainty about the future can bring about considerable negative and stressful feelings for an individual, which go on to affect their outer manifestations.

Now let's suppose that everything exists at a single point in time. Picture yourself in the middle of that black dot where the sum total of everything is happening at once. From this new vantage point of yours (which is also the Universe's perspective), you see everything playing out all at once—the past, present and future. In fact, there is no past, no present and no future because everything is happening *right now*, in this moment. From your new perspective, you see yourself both asking for whatever you want (in Phase 1) and also enjoying it (in Phase 3). You know with absolute certainty that what you ask for is already yours because the element of time and the "future" has been taken out of the equation and rendered irrelevant.

Suppose this is you, how would you feel?

What would you do?

Where would all those worry and doubtful feelings go?

That's right—it would be impossible for you to worry at all! All those negative feelings of doubt or fear would cease to exist once you had absolute certainty over what was happening in your "future." It's like worrying about the well-being of someone and having all that fear dissipate when you finally hear from that person. That dissipation of all negative thought is what you are going for here.

When you collapse and bring that future into now, all the worries, fears and negative feelings that previously sabotaged your manifestations cannot even exist. You do not have to make a conscious decision to stop worrying or drop all your negative feelings about the process. No willpower or discipline is needed. When you are living in a reality where you have absolute knowledge and evidence of your manifestations, then none of those negative feelings can even be held by you for a moment. This is the inner state that you should hold for spontaneous manifestations.

What I have described above is not merely a creative thinking exercise. It represents a true and real possibility, a completely new way of being and acting in this world. If spiritual masters throughout the ages have repeatedly shown us the timeless nature of the Universe and assured us of how we will always get what we ask for the moment we ask for it, then why are we still turning our backs on these possibilities and living in a way that runs contrary to these teachings? Why do we still trap ourselves by our limited and linear thinking of the manifestation process when these teachers and guides have shown us over and over again that our conventional understanding is not in line with how the Universe truly functions?

Perhaps now is the time to act in accordance with our new understanding of the Universe and to experience the world not from our limited, fearful human perspectives, but from the way the Universe sees it. After all, we are an integral part of this

Universe. Everything the spiritual masters (both in physical and non-physical form today) have taught up to this point is to support us in making this transition in consciousness. I invite you to join me as we explore this new way of being in the next chapter.

Chapter Nine
Understanding Zero

"Now that we *know* the truth, how can we *live* it?" This is a sentiment often echoed by students of these Universal principles. I have a somewhat different take on the question. My version of this question reads: "Now that we have *tasted* the truth, how can we continue living the old way? How can we hold on to the same outmoded beliefs that cause us to suffer needlessly?" Indeed, once we know what is truly possible and in store for us, living any other way will be a denial of our full creative abilities. Living in any lesser way will be placing a limitation on the totality of our wonderful human experience.

In each of my books, I have attempted to explain different ways to bridge the gap between theory and practice. "Theory" consists of the theoretical knowledge of *knowing* what is possible for you and "practice" represents the actual *living*—the actual experiencing of all this material. This book is no different. I have devoted the first portion of this book to explaining the underlying theories and laying the groundwork. Now is the time we can go on an experiential journey, knowing that we are all on the same page in terms of understanding.

Recall where we left off in the previous chapter. We ended the chapter by having you visualize (or draw) a black dot in the middle of a piece of white paper. This black dot symbolizes the sum total of all your experiences at a single point in time, with no distinction between the past, present and future. This black dot also represents the *zero point,* the infinite field of all possibilities. If you took the whole of the Universe and collapsed it into a single *zero* point, this would be it. The zero point encapsulates all that is possible, all that has been created and all that is in the process of becoming. It is the point from which everything originates.

When we talk about the zero point field or look at the little black dot that you have drawn on paper, it all seems so small and insignificant. What can that black dot, that zero point possibly contain? How can a single black dot, a single point in our time and space, possibly contain the sum total of all our experiences? And yet that is exactly what quantum physics has shown to be possible. A single point in the quantum energy field holds infinite, limitless potential that we can harness to become anything we want. More importantly, a single point represents the whole of the Universe, just as a drop of the ocean contains all of the original elements, in the same proportion, as the entire ocean.

The zero point represents the field of infinite possibilities, within which resides subsets of unrealized probabilities. In other words, we choose the realities that we want to experience from those infinite possibilities. It's like going to a buffet where there is every kind of food available and choosing those that we most like to eat. While we acknowledge that there are foods that we don't particularly like or care for, we also know that we are free to exercise our power of free choice in each moment and choose only those items that we like.

What we are going to do next is to tune your inner state to a place of alignment. Different spiritual teachers have different names for this. Abraham-Hicks (my favorite teachers) call this the experience of "getting into the Vortex." Others may call it letting go, or the process of allowing. No matter what you call it, I have found one thing to be true. When you are in a non-resistant, allowing inner state, then what you want comes very quickly on the outside. This is the state of instant and spontaneous manifestations. However, if you do not allow yourself to get into this state in the first place, then life seems like an ongoing struggle. You constantly notice things that make you feel bad. They stick out like a sore thumb in your everyday experience. You feel anxious and edgy, feeling the need to "change the world out there" in order to make yourself happy.

Let go of all that right now as you turn the page…

Chapter Ten

Creating Spontaneous Manifestations from Zero

Start by taking three deep breaths no matter where you are, exhaling slowly. There is no need to rush the process as we are not rushing to go anywhere. We are all ***here now***. Take more deep breaths, as many as you like, until you feel a sense of calmness and peace wash over you. Notice your increasing sense of relaxation and letting go as you read these words. Notice how light you feel on the inside as your thinking becomes softer. You are now placing yourself in a receptive, allowing state for the good to come into your life.

Just for now, think of one thing that you would like to manifest in your experience. It may be a tangible object or an intangible experience. Whatever it is, just gently bring that intention to mind right now, representing it in a form that is just right for you. Remember the Quick Statement process that you used earlier to identify one of your highest intentions? Or the statement that you used to summarize one of your highest desires? Now is a good time to bring that statement back to mind and just hold it gently in your conscious awareness.

Whenever we ask for something, it is always because we do not have it yet. We perceive it as a void in our current reality. Through the process of "asking," we hope that it can someday be a part of our future reality. When we think in such a linear fashion, we allow the intervening time between our present moment and the "future" moment to bring about various interfering thoughts of fear and worry. We may even start wondering *if* our manifestations will come true for us. All of this uncertainty adds stress and negative emotions to the manifestation process, which ironically delays and slows down our manifestations. Therefore, if there is a way to completely take our perception of "time" out of the equation, then all uncertainty would disappear in an instant and our manifestations (by virtue of Universal Law) will be a certainty for us. If there is a way to remove all negative emotions and doubts about the process, then our manifestations will happen quickly and spontaneously for us, with absolutely no fuss or delay.

As you hold the thought of what you want in your conscious awareness, gently notice how you have naturally intertwined it with the concept of time. Notice how you have represented it as taking place sometime in the future, somewhere down the road. Using your inner senses, <u>sense</u> which aspects of this intention signify that it is somewhere in the "future" and not happening right now? In other words, how do you know, as you think about this item, that it is a representation of something out there in the "future" and not now? You do not have to verbalize an answer but just sense the difference in your awareness.

Recall once again that the ability to pick out subtle differences is a crucial skill for deliberate manifestations. Pick an item that is currently in your physical reality. It may be your computer, your current car or your current home. Whatever it may be, choose an object that you currently possess. Bring that item to mind and notice how you represent it differently on the inside. Use your inner senses to quietly notice what is different between this object and what you currently desire.

For example, when I think of the car I'm currently driving, I notice that the thought feels physically closer to me when I think about it. Even without closing my eyes, I feel the thought form encroaching into my inner space, within 1 or 2 inches of my body the moment I think about my current car. When I think about a car I would *like to* own, that same sense of encroachment disappears. I am still thinking about that car, but now the thought no longer seems so close to me and within my personal space. The way each person perceives it will be different. Try this out with a few different object pairs, each time comparing your "future" desire to something that you currently own and notice the difference. This difference will be the key to removing the "time" element in your everyday manifestations. Once again, this is not a process to be rushed. You are not rushing to go anywhere, or to make anything happen, so take as much time as you like.

When you have identified the subtle differences in representation, take that supposedly "future" desire and represent it in the same way as something that you currently own. For example, I will take the thought of my future car and make it *feel as close as possible* to the thought form of my current car by feeling the thought encroaching into my personal space. How does it feel for you?

Notice what comes up immediately on doing so without trying to change any of it. Do you feel a sense of allowing and wellness, or is there an immediate sense of inner resistance? Some people may immediately feel a sick feeling in their gut, as if something is "not right." This feeling of rejection represents our unconscious resistance of whatever we have asked for. If we do not deal with these feelings of resistance in the now moment, then they are going to recur and continue to be an issue even if we somehow managed to physically manifest whatever we wanted.

I manifested my first car with a lot of forceful effort without first dealing with all the negative feelings, emotions and beliefs that were intertwined with the ownership of that car. I thought those emotions and beliefs would straighten themselves out once I owned the car. However, because I continued to hold on to some of those unresourceful beliefs at an unconscious level, owning that car only stirred up more of them, making me fearful and worried on a daily basis. I was always self-conscious when driving the car and worried about whether I could afford the repairs if it broke down. As a result, the car (ranked by J.D. Power as *the* most reliable car make of all time) broke down frequently and required expensive repairs! Can you see the power our unconscious thoughts and beliefs have in shaping our outer reality, even going *against* conventional prevailing wisdom? The moment I sorted out my inner beliefs and thoughts, the car started running like new again.

This is why it is important to deal with our unconscious beliefs and resistances to manifesting something *before* we manifest it in our experience. The manifestation process not only becomes easier and faster when we drop all of these extraneous opposing beliefs, the final physical manifestation becomes much more enjoyable and comfortable as well. Fortunately, there is no need to go through thorough psychoanalysis to drop any of your resistant feelings and thoughts. You can let them go easily—just like that.

Bring the thought of your future intention into the present and notice the spontaneous resistant feelings that come up for you. There is no need to fight or change them. Instead, use the letting go process that I have taught in several of my previous books (based on the Sedona Method by Lester Levenson):

(1) Can I let this resistant feeling go for now? Yes/No
(2) Will I let this resistant feeling go for now? Yes/No
(3) If so, when can I let this resistant feeling go?

Repeat this letting go process as many times as necessary *until* you feel the resistant feelings completely gone. It may be necessary to describe the resistant feeling more specifically. For example, you may ask: "Can I let this tension/fear/sense that I am kidding myself/my skepticism/my disbelief/my rejection go?" Go through several rounds of the process with one feeling at a time. Use whatever words that come up for you to accurately describe the sense of resistance. Check by again representing your "future" desire in present form and noticing the difference. If you feel completely free, congratulations! You have let go of your resistant feelings surrounding your intention. You are free.

Feel your intention *without* the presence of any intervening time. How does it feel? While you hold the intention, you also consciously know that it is something that exists in your living experience—right now. When something is part of your now, there can be no uncertainties, fears or worries about its existence. All uncertainties and limitations surrounding the manifestation would have been removed. Recognize how this feels like for you.

As you set this book down and go about your daily life, walk around with that feeling and knowingness still alive in you. You do not have to deliberately conjure up the feeling. All you have to do is to connect with this knowingness that is already there. What you have done in the above exercise is to align your way of understanding with the Universe's way (the truth). And because you cannot be living anything else other than the highest truth, then that truth already resides within you. You just have to become consciously aware of it. You just have to remember it as you go about your daily activities.

Let the Universe lead you on where to go next. You have already led the Universe by setting your highest intentions and placing your focus on the eternal truth. Now is the time for the Universe to unfold its many paths to you. As you go through the next few days or weeks with this inner knowingness still within you, look out for subtle signs and differences in your everyday experience. Gently and quietly notice what is different. Do not jump ahead of yourself by taking lackful actions. Let the Universe present itself to you. There is no need to tell anyone what you are doing in the hope that they will give you what you want, unless you feel truly inspired to do so. The shifts presented to you will hold the key to even greater adventures, in a way that is just right for you. There is nothing else you have to do. When you experience the past, present and future all at once, then you know that all is indeed well, and has always been well.

About The Author

Richard Dotts is a modern-day spiritual explorer. An avid student of ancient and modern spiritual practices, Richard shares how to apply these timeless principles in our daily lives. For more than a decade, he has experimented with these techniques himself, studying why they work and separating the science from the superstition. In the process, he has created successful careers as an entrepreneur, business owner, author and teacher.

Leading a spiritual life does not mean walking away from your current life and giving up everything you have. The core of his teachings is that you can lead a spiritual and magical life starting right now, from where you are, in whatever field you are in.

You can make a unique contribution to the world, because you are blessed with the abilities of a true creator. By learning how to shape the energy around you, your life can change in an instant, if you allow it to!

Richard is the author of more than 20 Amazon bestsellers on the science of manifestation and reality creation.

An Introduction to the Manifestations Approach of Richard Dotts

Even after writing more than 20 Amazon bestsellers on the subject of creative manifestations and leading a fulfilling life, Richard Dotts considers himself to be more of an adventurous spiritual explorer than a spiritual teacher or "master", as some of his readers have called him by.

"When you apply these spiritual principles in your own life, you will realize that everyone is a master, with no exceptions. Everyone has the power to design and create his own life on his own terms," says Richard.

"Therefore, there is no need to give up your power by going through an intermediary or any spiritual medium. Each time you buy into the belief that your good can only come through a certain teacher or a certain channel...you give up the precious opportunity to realize your own good. My best teachers were those who helped me recognize the innate power within myself, and kept the faith for me even when I could not see this spiritual truth for myself."

Due to his over-questioning and skeptical nature (unaided by the education which he received over the years), Richard struggled with the application of these spiritual principles in his early years.

After reading thousands of books on related subjects and learning about hundreds of different spiritual traditions with little success, Richard realized there was still one place left unexplored.

It was a place that he was the most afraid to look at: **his inner state.**

Richard realized that while he had been applying these Universal principles and techniques dutifully on the outside, his inner state remained tumultuous the whole time. Despite being well-versed in these spiritual principles, he was constantly plagued with negative feelings of worry, fear, disappointment, blame, resentment and guilt on the inside during his waking hours. These negative feelings and thoughts drained him of much of his energy and well-being.

It occurred to him that unless he was free from these negative feelings and habitual patterns of thought, any outer techniques he tried would not work. That was when he achieved his first spiritual breakthrough and saw improvements in his outer reality.

Taking A Light Touch

The crux of Richard's teachings is that one has to do the inner work first by tending to our own inner states. No one else, not even a powerful spiritual master, can do this for us. Once we have restored our inner state to a place of *zero*, a place of profound calmness and peace...that is when miracles can happen. Any subsequent intention that is held with a light touch in our inner consciousness quickly becomes manifest in our outer reality.

Through his books and teachings, Richard continually emphasizes the importance of taking a light touch. This means adopting a carefree, playful and detached attitude when working with these Universal Laws.

"Whenever we become forceful or desperate in asking for what we want, we invariably delay or withhold our own good. This is because we start to feel even more negative feelings of desperation and worry, which cloud our inner states further and prevent us from receiving what we truly want."

To share these realizations with others, Richard has written a series of books on various aspects of these manifestation principles and Universal Laws. Each of his books touches on a different piece of the manifestation puzzle that he has struggled with in the past.

For example, there are certain books that guide readers through the letting-go of negative feelings and the dropping of negative beliefs. There are books that talk about how to deal with self-doubt and a lack of faith in the application of these spiritual principles. Yet other books offer specific techniques for holding focused intentions in our inner consciousness. A couple of books deal with advanced topics such as nonverbal protocols for the manifestation process.

Richard's main goal is to break down the mysterious and vast subject of spiritual manifestations into easy to understand pieces for the modern reader. While he did not invent these Universal Laws and is certainly not the first to write about them, Richard's insights are valuable in showing readers how to easily apply these spiritual principles despite leading modern and hectic lifestyles. Thus, a busy mother of three or the CEO of a large corporation can just as easily access these timeless spiritual truths through Richard's works, as an ancient ascetic who lived quietly by himself.

It is Richard's intention to show readers that miracles are still possible in our modern world. When you experience the transformational power of these teachings for yourself, you stop seeing them as unexpected miracles and start seeing them as part of your everyday reality.

Do I have to read every book in order to create my own manifestation miracles?

Because Richard is unbounded by any spiritual or religious tradition, his work is continuously evolving based on a fine-tuning of his own personal experiences. He does, however, draw his inspiration from a broad range of teachings. Richard writes for the primary purpose of sharing his own realizations and not for any commercial interest, which is why he has shied away from the publicity that typically comes with being a bestselling author.

All of his books have achieved Amazon bestseller status with no marketing efforts or publicity, a testament to the effectiveness of his methods. An affiliation with a publishing house could mean a pressure to write books on certain popular subjects, or a need to censor the more esoteric and non-traditional aspects of his writing. Therefore, Richard has taken great steps to ensure his freedom as a writer. It is this freedom that keeps him prolific.

One of Richard's aims is to help readers apply these principles in their lives with minimal struggle or strain, which is why he has offered in-depth guidance on many related subjects. Richard himself has maintained that there is no need to read each and every single one of his books. Instead, one should just narrow in to the particular aspects that they are struggling with.

As he explains in his own words, "You can read just one book and completely change your life on the basis of that book if you internalized its teachings. You can do this not only with my books, but also with the books of any other author."

"For me, the journey took a little longer. One book could not do it for me. I struggled to overcome years of negative programming and critical self-talk, so much so that reading thousands of books did not help me as well. But after I reached that critical tipping point, when I finally 'got it', then I started to get everything. The first book, the tenth book, the hundredth book I read all started to make sense. I could pick up any book I read in the past and intuitively understand the spiritual essence of what the author was saying. But till I reached that point of understand within myself, I could not do so."

Therefore, one only needs to read as many books as necessary to achieve a true understanding on the inside. Beyond that, any reading is for one's personal enjoyment and for a fine-tuning of the process.

Which book should I start with?

There is no prescribed reading order. Start with the book that most appeals to you or the one that you feel most inspired to read. Each Richard Dotts book is self-contained and is written such that the reader can instantly benefit from the teachings within, no matter which stage of life they are at. If any prerequisite or background knowledge is needed, Richard will suggest additional resources within the text.

Other Books by Richard Dotts

Many of these titles are progressively offered in various formats (both in hard copy and eBook formats). Our intention is to eventually make all these titles available in hard copy format.

- **Banned Manifestation Secrets**
  It all starts here! In this book, Richard lays out the fundamental principles of spiritual manifestations and explains common misconceptions about the "Law of Attraction." This is also the book where Richard first talks about the importance of one's inner state in creating outer manifestations.
- **Come and Sit With Me (Book 1): How to Desire Nothing and Manifest Everything**
  If you had one afternoon with Richard Dotts, what questions would you ask him about manifesting your desires and the creative process? In Come and Sit With Me, Richard candidly answers some of the most pressing questions that have been asked by his readers. Written in a

free-flowing and conversational format, Richard addresses some of the most relevant issues related to manifestations and the application of these spiritual principles in our daily lives. Rather than shying away from tough questions about the manifestation process, Richard dives into them head-on and shows the readers practical ways in which they can use to avoid common manifestation pitfalls.

- **The Magic Feeling Which Creates Instant Manifestations**
  Is there really a "magic feeling", an inner state of mind that results in almost instant manifestations? Can someone live in a perpetual state of grace, and have good things and all your deepest desires come true spontaneously without any "effort" on your part? In this book, Richard talks about why the most effective part of visualizations lies in the *feelings*...and how to get in touch with this magic feeling.
- **Playing In Time And Space: The Miracle of Inspired Manifestations**
  In Playing In Time And Space, Richard Dotts shares the secrets to creating our own physical reality from our current human perspectives. Instead of seeing the physical laws of space and time as restricting us, Richard shares how anyone can transcend these perceived limitations of space and time by changing their thinking, and manifest right from where they are.

- **Allowing Divine Intervention**
  Everyone talks about wanting to live a life of magic and miracles, but what does a miracle really look like? Do miracles only happen to certain spiritual people, or at certain points in our lives (for example, at our most desperate)? Is it possible to lead an everyday life filled with magic, miracles and joy?

  In Allowing Divine Intervention, Richard explains how miracles and divine interventions are not reserved for the select few, but can instead be experienced by anyone willing to change their current perceptions of reality.
- **It is Done! The Final Step To Instant Manifestations**
  The first time Richard Dotts learnt about the significance of the word "Amen" frequently used in prayers…goosebumps welled up all over his body and everything clicked in place for him. Suddenly, everything he had learnt up to that point about manifestations made complete sense.

  In It Is Done!, Richard Dotts explores the hidden significance behind these three simple words in the English language. Three words, when strung together and used in the right fashion, holds the keys to amazingly accurate and speedy manifestations.
- **Banned Money Secrets**
  In Banned Money Secrets of the Hidden Rich, Richard explains how there is a group of

individuals in our midst, coming from almost every walk of life, who have developed a special relationship with money. These are the individuals for whom money seems to flow easily at will, which has allowed them to live exceedingly creative and fulfilled lives unlimited by money. More surprisingly, Richard discovered that there is not a single common characteristic that unites the "hidden rich" except for their unique ability to focus intently on their desires to the exclusion of everything else. Some of the "hidden rich" are the most successful multi-millionaires and billionaires of our time, making immense contributions in almost every field.

Richard teaches using his own life examples that the only true, lasting source of abundance comes from behaving like one of the hidden rich, and from developing an extremely conducive inner state that allows financial abundance to easily flow into your life.

- **The 95-5 Code: for Activating the Law of Attraction**

  Most books and courses on the Law of Attraction teach various outer-directed techniques one can use to manifest their desires. All is well and good, but an important question remains unanswered: What do you do during the remainder of your time when you are not actively using these manifestation techniques? How do you live? What do you do with the 95% of your day, the majority of your waking hours when you are not actively asking for what you want? Is the "rest of your day" important to the manifestation process?

It turns out that what you do during the 95% of your time, the time NOT spent visualizing or affirming, makes all of the difference.

In The 95-5 Code for activating the Law of Attraction, Richard Dotts explains why the way you act (and feel) during the majority of your waking hours makes all the difference to your manifestation end results.

- **Inner Confirmation for Outer Manifestations**
  How do you know if things are on their way after you have asked for them?

  What should you do after using a particular manifestation technique?

  What does evidence of your impending manifestations feel like?

  You may not have seen yourself as a particularly spiritual or intuitive person, much less an energy reader...but join Richard Dotts as he explains in Inner Confirmation for Outer Manifestations how everyone can easily perceive the energy fields around them.
- **Mastering the Manifestation Paradox**
  The Manifestation Paradox is an inner riddle that quickly becomes apparent to anyone who has been exposed to modern day Law of Attraction and manifestation teachings. It is an inner state that seems to be contradictory to the

person practicing it, yet one that is associated with inevitably fast physical manifestations—that of *wanting* something and yet at the same time *not wanting* it.

Richard Dotts explains why the speed and timing of our manifestations depends largely on our mastery of the Manifestation Paradox. Through achieving a deeper understanding of this paradox, we can consciously and deliberately move all our desires (even those we have been struggling with) to a "sweet spot" where physical manifestations *have to occur* very quickly for us instead of having our manifestations happen "by default."

- **Today I Am Free: Manifesting Through Deep Inner Changes**

  In Today I Am Free, Richard Dotts returns with yet another illuminating discussion of these timeless Universal Laws and spiritual manifestation principles. While his previous works focused on letting go of the worry and fear feelings that prevent our manifestations from happening in our lives, Today I Am Free focuses on a seldom discussed aspect of our lives that can affect our manifestations in a big way: namely our interaction with others and the judgments, opinions and perceptions that other people may hold of us. Richard Dotts shows readers simple ways in which they can overcome their constant feelings of fear and self-consciousness to be truly free.

- **Dollars Flow To Me Easily**
  Is it possible to read and relax your way into financial abundance? Can dollars flow to you even if you just sat quietly in your favorite armchair and did "nothing"? Is abundance and prosperity really our natural birthright, as claimed by so many spiritual masters and authors throughout the ages?

  Dollars Flow To Me Easily takes an alternative approach to answering these questions. Instead of guiding the reader through a series of exercises to "feel as if" they are already rich, Richard draws on the power of words and our highest intentions to dissolve negative feelings and misconceptions that block us from manifesting greater financial abundance in our lives.
- **Light Touch Manifestations: How To Shape The Energy Field To Attract What You Want**
  Richard covers the entire manifestation sequence in detail, showing exactly how our beliefs and innermost thoughts can lead to concrete, outer manifestations. As part of his approach of taking a light touch, Richard shows readers how to handle each component of the manifestation sequence and tweak it to produce fast, effective manifestations in our daily lives.
- **Infinite Manifestations: The Power of Stopping at Nothing**
  In Infinite Manifestations, Richard shares a practical, step-by-step method for erasing the unconscious memories and blocks that hold our

manifestations back. The Infinite Release technique, "revealed" to Richard by the Universe, is a quick and easy way to let go of any unconscious memories, blocks and resistances that may prevent our highest good from coming to us. When we invoke the Infinite Release process, we are no longer doing it alone. Instead, we step out of the way, letting go and letting God. We let Universal Intelligence decide how our inner resistances and blocks should be dissolved. All we need to do is to intend that we are clear from these blocks that hold us back. Once the Infinite Release process is invoked, it is done!

- **Let The Universe Lead You!**
  Imagine what your life would be like if you could simply hold an intention for something...and then be led clearly and precisely, every single time, to the fulfilment of your deepest desires. No more wondering about whether you are on the "right" path or making the "right" moves. No more second-guessing yourself or acting out of desperation—You simply set an intention and allow the Universe to lead you to it effortlessly!
- **Manifestation Pathways: Letting Your Good Be There...When You Get There!**
  Imagine having a desire for something and then immediately intuiting (knowing) what the path of least resistance should be for that desire. When you allow the Universe to lead you in this manner and unfold the manifestation pathway of least resistance to you, then life becomes as

effortless as knowing what you want, planting it in your future reality and letting your good be there when you get there...every single time! This book shows you the practical techniques to make it happen in your life.

- **And more...**

Made in the USA
San Bernardino, CA
20 February 2017